First World War
and Army of Occupation
War Diary
France, Belgium and Germany

29 DIVISION
87 Infantry Brigade
Devonshire Regiment
52nd Battalion
10 March 1919 - 31 October 1919

WO95/2305/5

The Naval & Military Press Ltd
www.nmarchive.com
Published in association with The National Archives

Published by

The Naval & Military Press Ltd

Unit 10 Ridgewood Industrial Park,

Uckfield, East Sussex,

TN22 5QE England

Tel: +44 (0) 1825 749494

www.naval-military-press.com

www.nmarchive.com

This diary has been reprinted in facsimile from the original. Any imperfections are inevitably reproduced and the quality may fall short of modern type and cartographic standards.

© Crown Copyright
Images reproduced by permission of The National Archives, London, England, 2015.

Contents

Document type	Place/Title	Date From	Date To
Heading	WO95/2305-5 52 Battalion Devonshire Regiment Mar 19-Oct 19		
Heading	Southern (Late 29th) Divn 87th Infy Bde 52nd Bn Devon Regt Mar-Oct 1919 To Independent Div Rhine Army		
War Diary	Dunkirk	10/03/1919	11/03/1919
War Diary	Cologne. Mulheim.	13/03/1919	13/03/1919
War Diary	Dunwald	14/03/1919	15/03/1919
War Diary	Borge	20/03/1919	20/03/1919
War Diary	Kellers Hammer.	29/03/1919	29/03/1919
War Diary	Burscheid	31/05/1919	31/05/1919
Operation(al) Order(s)	Alarm Orders. No I	03/05/1919	03/05/1919
Operation(al) Order(s)	Battalion Order No. 2 a. Issued on Receipt of Brigade Order No. 2 of 9/5/1919.	09/05/1919	09/05/1919
Operation(al) Order(s)	Battalion Order No. 3 Of 9/5/1919.	09/05/1919	09/05/1919
Miscellaneous	Defensive Action. No 2	09/05/1919	09/05/1919
Operation(al) Order(s)	Battalion Order No. 4 2nd Southern Infantry Brigade Order No. 5.	27/05/1919	27/05/1919
Operation(al) Order(s)	Administrative Instructions To Accompany Battalion Operation Order No. 4. Brigade Order No. 5	22/05/1919	22/05/1919
Operation(al) Order(s)	Battalion Order No. 4 2nd. Southern Infantry Brigade Order No. 5.	27/05/1919	27/05/1919
Miscellaneous	Battalion Order No 4 (Amendment).		
War Diary	Burscheid.	11/06/1919	14/06/1919
War Diary	Dellbruck.	17/06/1919	17/06/1919
War Diary	Burscheid.	19/06/1919	19/06/1919
War Diary	Solingen.	23/06/1919	30/06/1919
War Diary	Burscheid.	11/06/1919	14/06/1919
War Diary	Dellbruck.	17/06/1919	17/06/1919
War Diary	Burscheid.	19/06/1919	19/06/1919
War Diary	Solingen.	23/06/1919	30/06/1919
Operation(al) Order(s)	52nd. Battalion The Devonshire Regiment. Operation Order No. 5.	23/06/1919	23/06/1919
War Diary	Burscheid	01/07/1919	04/07/1919
War Diary	Dellbruck.	05/07/1919	12/07/1919
War Diary	Burg	28/07/1919	28/07/1919
War Diary	Urscheid	01/07/1919	04/07/1919
War Diary	Ellbruck.	05/07/1919	12/07/1919
War Diary	Urg	28/07/1919	28/07/1919
War Diary	Burscheid	01/07/1919	04/07/1919
War Diary	Dellbruck.	05/07/1919	12/07/1919
War Diary	Burg	28/07/1919	27/09/1919
Miscellaneous	52nd. Battalion The Devonshire Regiment. Move To Hilgen.		
War Diary	Hilgen	21/10/1919	28/10/1919
War Diary	Burscheid	31/10/1919	31/10/1919
Miscellaneous	52nd. Battalion The Devonshire Regiment. Battalion Move 31/10/19.	31/10/1919	31/10/1919
Miscellaneous	Alarm Orders.		

Miscellaneous	52nd Battalion The Devonshire Regiment. Movement Orders.		
Miscellaneous	52nd Battalion The Devonshire Regiment. Move. Alarm Orders. (Amendment)	20/10/1919	20/10/1919
Miscellaneous			

WO/95/2305/5

5/2 Battentin Dorsetslire Regiment

Mar'19 - Oct '19

SOUTHERN (LATE 29TH) DIVN
87TH INFY BDE

52ND BN DEVON REGT
OCT
MAR-~~DEC~~ 1919

~~To H.Q. Div Rhine~~

TO INDEPENDENT DIV
RHINE ARMY

Army Form C. 2118.

Durham (?)

WAR DIARY
or
INTELLIGENCE SUMMARY.
(Erase heading not required.)

52nd Bn. Devon Regt.

Page 1

Mar – Dec 1919

Place	Date	Hour	Summary of Events and Information	Remarks and references to Appendices
DUNKIRK	10/3/19	12.15	The Battalion landed at DUNKIRK and marched to the Rest Camp for the purpose of resting the night there.	
do	11/3/19	10.30	The Battalion entrained at DUNKIRK, and proceeded to COLOGNE.	
COLOGNE (Mulheim)	12/3/19	07.30	Arrived at Cologne MULHEIM Railway Stn, detrained & marched to DÜNWALD where the Battalion was accommodated in billets.	
DÜNWALD	14/3/19	08.40	Advance Party left by motor lorries for SCHLOSS Burg, to take over from 1st K.O.S.B. E" Coy. also proceeded to take over from Buffar Coy. for (K.O.S.B).	
do	15/3/19	08.30	The Battalion (less advance party) marched to COLOGNE MULHEIM Rly Stn. and entrained. Detrained at WERMELSKIRCHEN, and marched to SCHLOSS BURG. The Bn. was accommodated as follows. Headquarters and "A" Coy. in the Schloss. "B" Coy. " "C" Coy. in houses outside the Schloss. "D" Coy. " "E" Coy. in houses at UNTER BURG. in houses at WIERINGHAUSEN, on outpost Duty, with one platoon (8/Lt. G.H. Befsen) on duty at THE HATCHERIES POST. (KELLERS HAMMER)	

Army Form C. 2118.

WAR DIARY
INTELLIGENCE SUMMARY

(Erase heading not required.)

52nd Bn. Devon Regt.

Page 2.

Place	Date	Hour	Summary of Events and Information	Remarks and references to Appendices
BORG	20/6/19	11.00	Battalion inspected by G.O.C. Southern Division.	
KELLERS HAMMER	29/6/19	12.00	One Platoon "E" Coy. (2/Lt. G.H. Brown) relieved by one Platoon "C" Coy. Lieut. C.W. Pamplin.	

N. Adams
Lieut. Colonel,
Comdg. 52nd Bn. Devonshire Regt.

Army Form C. 2118.

WAR DIARY
INTELLIGENCE SUMMARY.
(Erase heading not required.)

Place	Date	Hour	Summary of Events and Information	Remarks and references to Appendices
BURSCHEID	31st May 1919	—	Battalion still billetted in BURSCHEID and KUCKENBURG. ("B" Company in the latter village.) During the month "A" and "B" Companies have established their own minature Ranges; a 300 yard open range has been made and is now in use for A.R.A. Competitions as well as ordinary range practices; A live bombing ground is in the course of erection. ATTACHED ARE SPECIAL AND OPERATION ORDERS No. 1, 2, 2a, 3 and 4 ISSUED DURING THE MONTH.	

BURSCHEID.
1-6-1919.

Captain and Adjutant,
52nd Bn THE DEVONSHIRE REGIMENT.
for Lt.Col. Comdg.

ALARM ORDERS.

In the event of a Rising or Serious disturbance on the part of civilian population the following action will be taken.

1. a. The "Alarm" will be sounded by Battalion Headquarter Bugler on duty and repeated by all Company Buglers who hear it.

   b. A cyclist orderly will be sent at once to each Company to carry the Alarm.

   c. Troops will fall in outside their billets – Dress F.S.M.O.

2. O.C. "A" Company will detail the following guards:-

   1. Lewis Gun Section
   1. Rifle Section   BURSCHEID RAILWAY STATION.

   1. Rifle Section   POST OFFICE.

   1. Rifle Section   WATER TOWER.

   1. Rifle Section
   1. Lewis Gun Section   BURGOMASTERS OFFICE BURSCHEID.

   1. Rifle Section   BATTALION QUARTERMASTERS STORES AND ORDERLY ROOMS.

   1. Rifle Section   TRANSPORT LIMBERS BURSCHEID CHURCH.

   O.C. "B" Company will detail:-

   1. Lewis Gun Section
   1. Rifle Section   KUCKENBERG RAILWAY STATION AND COMPANY STORES.

   ---

3. a. All German Officials will be forced to remain at their posts and carry on with their duties under supervision.

   b. All civilians will be confined to their houses by order of the Burgomaster. Any Civilian found in the streets without a pass signed by O.C. Troops is to be arrested.

   c. The movement of trains and trams will be stopped.

   d. Guards will be placed on all food and wine stores and any person attempting looting will be fired on. The Burgomaster will arrange for the proper distribution of food.

   e. Guards will be placed on all Quarter Master's Stores and on all buildings in which rifles or ammunition are stored.

   f. Lewis Guns will be placed in positions commanding all main thoroughfares.

   g. Transport will be concentrated near BURSCHEID church.

-2-

4. O.C. "A" "B" and "D" Company are responsible that the orders in para. 3. a to f. are carried out within the areas as shown on the attached map. O.C. "B" Company is responsible that these orders are carried out within Company billeting area. M.T.O. will arrange for compliance with para. f 3.

"C" Company will be ready to move at short notice.

5. One Officer from each Company accompanied by an Orderly will report immediately at Battalion Headquarters.

6. On hearing the "ALARM" or on receipt of the message "BOLSHEVISM" take action" - Action as detailed above will be taken.

Burscheid.

3/5/1919.

M. Herbert.
Capt.
Adjutant.
2nd. Bn. Devonshire Regt.

War Diary

BATTALION ORDER NO. 2 a., ISSUED ON RECEIPT OF BRIGADE ORDER
NO. 2 of 9/5/1919.

Reference sheet 2/K 1/1.00000. REMSCHEID _ BURSCHEID 1/25000.

------------------oOo------------

"HOSTILITIES" MOVE 10-00 a.m. 10th. instant and.
Patrols and Guards as detailed will move and take parts
forthwith and acknowledge.

A copy of Battalion order No. 2 to which the code word
HOSTILITIES refers is attached.

------------oOo------------

Burscheid.
5/5/1919.

War Diary

BATTALION ORDER NO. 3 OF 9/5/1919.

References, RAMSCHEID - HURSCHEID 1/25,000. Sheet 2 K 1/100,000

Reference Brigade Order No. 3.

i. The Allied Armies are advancing into the interior of Germany commencing to-morrow May 10th.

ii. The 2nd. Southern Brigade will advance along the route - BURG - REMSCHEID - BARMEN - HASSLINGHAUSEN - GRUNDSCHOTTEL - VOLMARSTIEN - WESTHOFEN - SCHWERTE - HANGSEN.

The 1st. XXX. and 3rd. Southern Brigades are co-operating on the left and right respectively of the 2nd. Brigade.

iii. The Advanced Guard is composed as under:-

O.C. Lieut. Col. H.L. Dobbin, D.S.O.
   51st. Devonshire Regiment.
   2 Sect. M. G. Company.
   1 Sect. L.T.M.B.

IV. Main Body in order of march is composed as under:-

   Brigade Headquarters,
   5th. Devons (less three Companies.)
   Battery R.F.A.
   B Company M.G.C. (less 2 Sections.)
   3 Companies 5 th. Devon Regiment.
   2nd. Sthn. L.T.M.B. (less one section)
   D. 4.5. Battalion 113 Brigade R.F.A.
   52nd. Battalion Devonshire Regiment.
   (Less one platoon.)
   2 Section 87th. Field Company.
   Ambulance.
   No. 3 Company Train.-

V. The 52nd. Battalion Devonshire Regiment. Order of March as under:-

Battalion Headquarters,
A.
C.   Starting point HURSCHEID CHURCH.
D.   Time. 06-25 a.m. 10th. Apl.
B.   ROUTE. HURSCHEID - HILGER.

B Transport   Distances:- F.S.R. Sectn. 25.
Dress, F.S.M.O.

VI. TRANSPORT :-
Battalion Transport will march in rear of the Battalion under orders of Battalion Transport Officer.
Lewis Gun Limbers leading in order of Companies.

VII. Rear Guard.
O.C. "B" Company will detail one platoon to act as rear guard to the 2nd. Brigade. (F.S.R. para. 74.)

VIII. Administrative Instructions are attached.

IX Reports to Head of the Battalion.

SECRET.

DEFENSIVE ACTION.   No 2

Reference sheet B.K. 1/100,000.

BOUNDERIES.

1. The Boundories of the Brigade Sector are shown on attached map.

DEFENSIVE SYSTEM.

2. The defensive system comprises the following:-

   a. The Outpost on Perimeter line,
   b. Line of Resistance ----- The HUNGER -BURG Line. Comprising the defended localities of HUNGER and BURG.

NOTES. 1. WERMELSKIRCHEN is held by the Brigade on the Right.

2. The line of resistance of the Brigade on the left approximate to the perimeter line viz, the line of the WUPPER River from HUNGSTEIN Northwards.

   c. The 2nd. Line of defence, Defended localities at DABRINGHAUSEN - HILGEN - WITZHELDEN - KOHLSBERG - RICHRATH.

DISPOSITIONS.

3. The Present dispositions of the Brigade Group is as follows:-
   A Battalion outpost duties. Battalion Headquarters BURG.

   B Battalion. HILGEN.

   C Battalion. BURSCHEID,

   1. Battery 18 Pdr. BERG GLADBACH.

   1. Battery 4.5 Hows WITZHELDEN.

   Field Company R.E.
   T. M. B.   BURSCHEID.
   Brigade Headquarters

   M. G. Company. DABRINGHAUSEN.

ACTION.

4. In the event of hostile attack threatened or commenced The 52nd. Battalion Devonshire Regiment ("C" Battalion) less one platoon and one section will move to the CROSS BRUCH - HILGEN area with Battalion Headquarters at HILGEN.

   Starting Point.   CHURCH BURSCHEID.

   Orders of march:- Battalion Headquarters,
                      A Company,
                      C   "
                      D   "
                      Transport,
                      B Company.

   Dress, F. S. M. O. --- 100 yards distance between Coys.

   O. C. "A" Company will detail one platoon as follows:-

1 Rifle and 1 Lewis Gun Section.

To patrol the BURSCHEID – WERMELSKIRCHEN Railway between HILGEN and KUCKENBERG Railway Stations both inclusive.

1 Rifle Section.

To report to N. C. O. in charge Brigade Headquarters Signal Office (Post Office BURSCHEID) for the purpose of protecting telephone exchanges.

1 Rifle Section.

To report at Battalion Quarter Master's Stores and form a Guard thereon.

O. C. "B" Company will detail:-

1 Rifle Section.

As Guard on stores KUCKENBURG Railway Station.

STORES ETC.

Company Stores, surplus kit etc. will be concentrated as under:-

A. C. D. Companies Battalion Quarter Master's Stores.

B Company. KUCKENBURG Railway Station.

(NOTE:- B Company Stores will be brought in to Battalion Quarter Master's Stores first available opportunity.)

DISPOSITION.

5. Headquarters of neighbouring formations will be as under:-

Brigade Headquarters   H I L G E N.

A Battalion.
D Battalion.   OBERWINKEL – HAUSEN.

R. H. A.
M. G. Company   Near OBERWINKEL – HAUSEN.

COMMUNICATION.

A Brigade Headquarters Transmitting Station will be established near HEID Cross Roads ½ Mile from HILGEN on HILGEN – EITZHELDON Road.

CODE WORD.

On receipt of the message "Hostilities" Move 00.00.

Action as detailed above will be taken. Companies and patrols will be ready to move off and Guards mounted by the hour stated.

****

Burscheid.
9/5/1919.

War Diary

BATTALION ORDER NO. 4

2nd. SOUTHERN INFANTRY BRIGADE ORDER NO. 5.

Reference Germany. Sheets 55 and 59

1. (a) The enemy has refused to sign the Peace Terms and the Armistice therefore ends on a day known as J day on which date hostilities re-open.

   (b) On J day the allied armies will advance with a view to seizing as rapidly as possible FRANKENBERG, SOEST and Ham, by American, British and Belgian respectively.

   (c) The first *objective* of the British Army is the Railway running S.E. from HAGEN.
   This objective will be made good by the VIth. Corps who will move forward in lorries on J day via WERMELSKIRCHEN – LENNEP – SCHWELM – HAGEN followed by a Cavalry Division.

   The 11 Corps will operate in conjunction with the VIth. Corps, moving by route march.
   The final areas to be occupied by the 11 Corps will be approximately
   Southern Division:- UNNA – HAGEN – WITTEN (exclusive).

   Lowland Division:- GEVELSBERG – RONSDORF – DUSSELDORF – HATTINGEN (exclusive).

   (d) On (J – 1) day the 1st. Brigade is concentrating at BURSCHEID and the 3rd. Brigade at BURG.

2. The 2nd. Brigade group-composition as under will concentrate at SOLINGEN on (J – 1) day.
   G.O.C. 2nd.Sth. Inf. Bde. 2nd. Southern Infantry Bde.
   B/113 Batt. R.F.A., D/113 Batt. R.F.A. (Howitzers). A Company
   29th. Batt. M.G.C., A Coy. 9th. Gloucesters, 1 section F.A. (P).
   No. 3 Coy. Div. Train.

3. The move to SOLINGEN will be conducted as follows:-
   (a) BURSCHEID Column.   *1/25000 map*
   Starting point will be the cross roads just north of "H" in BURSCHEID.

UNIT.	Pass Starting Point at	ROUTE.
Brigade H.Q. less Transport.	X hours	BURSCHEID.
P.R.O. with Police,	"	(1/25000 map).
2nd. Southern L.T.M.B.	X hours plus 1 min.	PAFFENLOH.-
52nd.Devons, less Transport	X hours plus 2 min.	-WITZHELDON.-
"A" Coy. 9th. Gloucesters,	X hours plus 6 min.	-SOLINGEN.

   (b) HILGEN Column.
   Starting point will be cross roads about point E 4.86.

UNIT.	Pass starting point at.	ROUTE.
5th. Devons.	X hour plus 60 min.	HILGEN –
Transport Bde. H.Q.	X hour plus 69 min.	– WERMELSKIRCHEN –
Transport L.T.M.B.	X hour plus 70 min.	BURG - SOLINGEN.
Transport 52nd.Devons,	X hour plus 71 min.	
No. 3 Div. Train,	X hour plus 74 min.	

4. DRESS. Fighting order – Packs carried on Lorries. Haversack rations will be carried.

5. Companies will report their arrival in billets, stating location, and number of men who have fallen out on the march.

6. Company Commanders will ensure that foot inspection takes place at the conclusion of each day's march.

7. No bridge guard or Guards on Civil buildings will be left by Units of the Brigade Group in the Sub area.

8. J day and X hour will be notified later.

CONTINUED:- - 2. -

9. Administrative instructions will be issued separately.
10. ACKNOWLEDGE.

                                      E.W. Hebbert Capt. for Major, for
                                                                               Lieut. Col.
BURSCHEID.   Commanding 52nd. BATTALION THE DEVONSHIRE REGT.
27th. May 1919.

Issued at 1700 hours PM.

Copy to Commanding Officer,
"   "   Adjutant,
"   "   "A" Company.
"   "   "B"   "
"   "   "C"   "
"   "   "D"   "
"   "   Headquarters Company.
"   "   Transport Officer
"   "   Quartermaster,
"   "   War Diary,
"   "   File.

                    ****

The following maps are sent out to all Coys with these orders.

6 Sheets	Germany	3. S. N.W.
"	"	3. S. N.E.
"	"	3. S. S.E.
"	"	2. S. S.W
"	"	2. S. S.E.
1	"	56
1	"	55
1	"	59
1	"	60

Please acknowledge receipt.

ADMINISTRATIVE INSTRUCTIONS TO ACCOMPANY BATTALION OPERATION ORDER
No. 4., BRIGADE ORDER No. 5 of 22/5/1919.
=====================

1. DUMPS. All Government Stores not taken forward, blankets, etc, will be dumped at Divisional Dump, MULHEIM on receipt of instructions. Lorries for this purpose have been requisitioned. It is expected that one will be provided to make two trips. No Regimental or private property must be dumped with these stores as in all probability the Government Stores will be pooled for General re-issue.
Other stores and surplus baggage will be stored at Brigade Dump, HILGEN (in school room at NUNHAUSEN) under direct charge of unit representatives.
Battalion will commence this storing as soon as definite orders are issued.
No blankets will be stored there except those necessary for the bundling of Kits.
"D" Company will provide 1 N.C.O. and 2 men to remain behind at this HILGEN dump as part of a Guard being provided by units of the Brigade.
"B" Company will provide the representative Officer to assist in the supervision of Battalion Dumping. This Orderly Room to be informed of Officer chosen.
A full list of stores dumped is to be prepared in triplicate, one copy to Brigade, one to Dump and one to Unit.

2. BAGGAGE. Transport will be limited to 2 Motor Vans per Infantry Battalion (which will carry men's packs) together with 1st. line Transport and baggage wagons of 2nd. line Transport. Baggage wagons will always accompany first line behicles. All regulation first line loads will be taken. Battalion will move with Mob. stores complete. No blankets will be taken. Great coats in packs on lorries. Ammunition will be made up to 120 rounds per man. Companies will make necessary arrangements with Quartermaster forthwith.
Practice munitions will NOT be carried forward.
Loading of wagons to be supervised by Battalion Transport Officer. Wagons will be inspected on route under Divisional arrangements and all cases of overloading will be dealt with by immediate dumping irrespective of goods so dumped, and those goods will be lost to units until and unless rescued by salvage.

3. ADVANCE PARTIES. Billeting parties of 1 Officer (Lt. Baylor), 4 C.Q.M.Sergeants and 1 N.C.O. for Headquarters Company, will proceed at head of column daily when moving. They will rendezvous with the Staff Captain as detailed on each occasion.
Advance party will meet Staff Captain at Burgomeisters Office, Solingen on J - 1 day at hour to be given later. Name of Headquarter Company N.C.O. to be rendered forthwith.

4. BILLETTING AND QUARTERING. During concentration at SOLINGEN it is possible that troops will have to bivouac in the open. It is pointed out, however, that Rules prohibiting the occupation of schools, vicarages, factories etc. will be in abeyance from the moment of starting.

5. REAR PARTIES. Any rear parties left behind - such as a dump guard, or any guard dropped on the march to guard important points, - will be left with 3 days rations, After that date rations will be drawn on Sub-area Commandant, "Highland Division."

6. MAPS, GERMANY, SHEETS 55 and 59 in connection with these operations are attached herewith.

7. ACKNOWLEDGE.

U. Herbert Capt for Major for Lieut. Col.
BURSCHEID.Commanding 52nd. BATTALION THE DEVONSHIRE REGIMENT.
27/5/1919.
Issued at 1700 hrs

Copies to:- Commanding Officer, Adjutant, "A", "B", "C", "D", and Headqr. Companies, Transport Officer, Quartermaster, War Diary, File.

For war diary [signature]

BATTALION ORDER NO. 4

2nd. SOUTHERN INFANTRY BRIGADE ORDER NO. 5.

Reference Germany sheets 55 and 59

1. (a) The enemy has refused to sign the Peace Terms and the Armistice therefore ends on a day known as J day on which date hostilities re-open.

   (b) On J day the allied armies will advance with a view to seizing as rapidly as possible FRANKENBERG, SOEST and Ham, by American, British and Belgian respectively.

   (c) *objective* The first of the British Army is the Railway running S.E. from HAGEN.
   This objective will be made good by the VIth. Corps who will move forward in lorries on J day via WERMELSKIRCHEN - LENNEP - SCHWELM - HAGEN followed by a Cavalry Division.

   The 11 Corps will operate in conjunction with the VIth. Corps, moving by route march.
   The final areas to be occupied by the 11 Corps will be approximately
   Southern Division:- UNNA - HAGEN - WITTEN (exclusive).

   Lowland Division:- GEVELSBERG - RONSDORF - DUSSELDORF - HATTINGEN (exclusive).

   (d) On (J - 1) day the 1st. Brigade is concentrating at BURSCHEID and the 3rd. Brigade at BURG.

2. The 2nd. Brigade group-composition as under will concentrate at SOLINGEN on (J - 1) day.
   G.O.C. 2nd. Sth. Inf. Bde. 2nd. Southern Infantry Bde.
   B/113 Batt. R.F.A., D/113 Batt. R.F.A. (Howitzers). A Company 29th. Batt. M.G.C., A Coy. 9th. Gloucesters, 1 section F.A. (P).
   No. 3 Coy. Div. Train.

3. The move to SOLINGEN will be conducted as follows:-
   (a) BURSCHEID Column.   *1/25000 map*
   Starting point will be the cross roads just north of "H" in BURSCHEID.

UNIT.	Pass Starting Point at	ROUTE.
Brigade H.Q. less Transport.	X hours	BURSCHEID.
P.R.O. with Police,	"	(1/25000 map).
2nd. Southern L.T.M.B.	X hours plus 1 min.	PAFFENLOH.-
52nd. Devons, less Transport	X hours plus 2 min.	-WITZHELDEN.-
"A" Coy. 9th. Gloucesters,	X hours plus 6 min.	-SOLINGEN.

   (b) HILGEN Column.
   Starting point will be cross roads about point E 4.60.

UNIT.	Pass starting point at.	ROUTE.
5th. Devons.	X hour plus 60 min.	HILGEN -
Transport Bde. H.Q.	X hour plus 69 min.	- WERMELSKIRCHEN -
Transport L.T.M.B.	X hour plus 70 min.	BURG - SOLINGEN.
Transport 52nd. Devons,	X hour plus 71 min.	
No. 3 Div. Train,	X hour plus 74 min.	

4. DRESS. Fighting order - Packs carried on Lorries. Haversack rations will be carried.

5. Companies will report their arrival in billets, stating location, and number of men who have fallen out on the march.

6. Company Commanders will ensure that foot inspection takes place at the conclusion of each day's march.

7. No bridge guard or Guards on Civil buildings will be left by Units of the Brigade Group in the Sub area.

8. J. day and X hour will be notified later.

CONTINUED:- - 2. -

9. Administrative instructions will be issued separately.

10. ACKNOWLEDGE.

C.M. Hebbert
Capt. for
Major, for
Lieut. Col.

BURGCHEID. Commanding 52nd. BATTALION THE DEVONSHIRE REGT.
27th. May 1919.

Issued at _1700 hours_.

Copy to Commanding Officer,
" "   Adjutant,
" "   " A " Company.
" "   " B "   "
" "   " C "   "
" "   " D "   "
" "   Headquarters Company.
" "   Transport Officer
" "   Quartermaster,
" "   War Diary,
" "   File.

****

War Diary

9

BATTALION ORDER NO. 4. (Amendment).

Reference Sheets 55 and 59, Germany.

The following alterations and additions to Battalion Order No. 4 of 27th. May 1919 are now in force.

"J" day is June 20th.
"X" hour will be 09-00 hours.

3. (a) BURSCHEID column will be under Command of Officer Commanding 52nd. Battalion The Devonshire Regiment.
Order of march of 52nd. Devons:-

Battalion Headquarters,
"A" Company.
"C" Company,
"D" Company,
"B" Company.

Band will be distributed by Sergeant Norris as stretcher bearers amongst Companies, Instruments dumped at Battalion dump, HILGEN. Head of Column by Battalion Headquarters, facing East, Battalion will move forward for starting point (see 3(a)) at 08-45 hours 100 Yards between Companies.

(b) HILGEN Column, under Command of O.C. 51st. Devons.

52nd. Devon Transport will pass starting point (see 3 b.) at 10-15 hours A.M. and not as previously stated.

Watches will be synchronised on evening of J-2 days for which purpose one Officer per Company, Scout Officer, Signalling Officer and Transport Officer will meet at Battalion Headquarters. Time will be given later.

General "G" Instructions for an Advance are attached herewith.

ACKNOWLEDGE.

CM Hebbert
Captain and Adjutant,
52nd. BATTALION THE DEVONSHIRE REGT.

Copy No. 1. to Commanding Officer,
"   "   2. " Adjutant,
"   "   3. " Quarter Master,
"   "   4. " Transport Officer,
"   "   5. " Signalling Officer,
"   "   6. " Scout Officer,
"   "   7. " Officer Commanding Companies,
"   "   8. " File,
"   "   9. " War Diary.

Issued at _____ hours.

A.F. C. 2118.

WAR DIARY.

Place.	Date.	hour.	Summary of events and information.
BURSCHEID.	11/6/1919.		Major G.E.R. Prior, D.S.O., M.C., proceeded to England to join his Battalion.
"	14/6/1919.		The Battalion marched from BURSCHEID to DELLBRUCK this morning for Annual Musketry Course, and is now encamped there. Firing commenced with a "Tracer Bullet" demonstration at 17-30 hours to-day.
DELLBRUCK.	17/6/1919.		Orders received by telegram at 08-30 hours to-day to return forthwith to BURSCHEID ready for possible advance into GERMANY. Arrived BURSCHEID at 15-30 hours to occupy same billets as before.
BURSCHEID.	19/6/1919.		Marched to SOLINGEN, and arrived there at 12-30 hours, billetted in Northern edge of town.
SOLINGEN.	23/6/1919.	16-00 hrs.	Received news that Germany agreed to accept Peace Terms. Operation Order No. 5 issued to-day.
"	28/6/1919.	18-00 hrs.	News was received that Peace Terms were signed at VERSAILLES to-day.
"	30/6/1919.		The Battalion will move back to BURSCHEID to-morrow morning, 1st July. Copies of:- Ammendment to Operation Order 4, and Operation Order 5 attached herewith.

Adjutant,
2nd. Bn. Devonshire Regt.

A.F. C. 2118.

WAR DIARY.

Place.	Date.	hour.	Summary of events and information.
BURSCHEID.	11/6/1919.		Major G.E.R. Prior, D.S.O., M.C., proceeded to England to join his Battalion.
"	14/6/1919.		The Battalion marched from BURSCHEID to DELLBRUCK this morning for Annual Musketry Course, and is now encamped there. Firing commenced with a "Tracer Bullet" demonstration at 17-30 hours to-day.
DELLBRUCK.	17/6/1919.		Orders received by telegram at 08-30 hours to-day to return forthwith to BURSCHEID ready for possible advance into GERMANY. Arrived BURSCHEID at 15-30 hours to occupy same billets as before.
BURSCHEID.	19/6/1919.		Marched to SOLINGEN, and arrived there at 12-30 hours, billetted in Northern edge of town.
SOLINGEN.	23/6/1919.	16-00 hrs.	Received news that Germany agreed to accept Peace Terms. Operation Order No. 5 issued to-day.
"	28/6/1919.	18-00 hrs.	News was received that Peace Terms were signed at VERSAILLES to-day.
"	30/6/1919.		The Battalion will move back to BURSCHEID to-morrow morning, 1st.July. Copies of :- Amendment to Operation Order 4, and Operation Order 5 attached herewith.

V. Ritchie A/Adjutant
52nd. Bn. Devonshire Reg.

War Diary

52nd. BATTALION THE DEVONSHIRE REGIMENT. OPERATION ORDER NO. 5.
Copy No. 10 . Reference Sheet 59.1/200,000 .

1. a. The Advance into the Interior of Germany will commence on a day to be known as "J" day.

   b. The 3rd. Southern Brigade marches to RONDORF and LUTHRINGHAUSEN via REMSCHEID.

   c. One Brigade Lowland Division (15th. H.L.I. Advance Guard) moves to ELBERFELD and Point 291 via VOHWINKEL.

2. The 2nd. Southern Brigade Group will move to BARMEN and point 301 North of BARMEN.

   ROUTE:- SOLINGEN - CRONENBERG - right hand road to BARMEN keeping South of both ELBERFELD - BARMEN Railways.

3. The 52nd. Devonshire Regiment will form Advance Guard which will be composed as under in order of march, and establish a line of outposts as follows:-

   From bend of WUPPER River just East of N in Barmen round Eastern and Northern edge of BARMEN to road running Southward through K in GENNEBRUCK.

   VAN GUARD. (O.C. Captain A.F. Mills, M.C.)

   1 Section 4th. Corps. Cyclists.   "C" Coy. Lewis Gun limber
   "C" Company.   will march in rear of the
   1 Section 2nd. Southern Brigade L.T.M.B. Company, together with
                                             Pack Animals.

   MAIN GUARD. (Lieut. Col. A.B.Incledon-Webber,C.M.G.,D.S.O.)

   1 Section 4th.Corps.Cyclists.   Will move 400 yards in
   "B" Company.   rear of Van Guard.
   "D" Company.   Distances 50 yards
   "A" Company.   between Units.
   Lewis Gun Limbers) Less "C" Coy. L.G.
   Pack Animals   ) limber & Packs.
   2 Sections M.G.C.

4. STARTING POINT. Junction of KULLER STR. - CRONENBERGER STR. at an hour to be notified later. The point of Advance Guard will maintain a position 40 minutes ahead of the Main Body, i.e., about 2,500 yards.

5. TRANSPORT. Remainder of Battalion Transport will be Brigaded and march under order of Brigade T.O.
   Battalion T.O. will arrange to draw up his Transport on right of road at Starting Point STOCKERBERG ready to join the Transport Column in its correct position.

6. BILLETING PARTY. 1 N.C.O. per Company will report to Lieut. Baylor at Starting Point and will move immediately in rear of the Advanced Guard.

2nd. BATTALION THE DEVONSHIRE REGIMENT. OPERATION ORDER NO. 5.
Copy No._____.   Reference Sheet 09. 1/200,000.

- 2 -

7. DISPOSITIONS.

On clearing BARMEN.

a. "C" Company will occupy outpost line from Point East of H in BARMEN. (East of River) to Railway line at "H" in SCHWELM exclusive.

b. "B" Company will occupy outpost line from Railway line at H in SCHWELM inclusive to road running Southward to K in GRUNEBRUCK.

Main roads will be picquetted and intervening Country patrolled. Vehicles will be examined for Arms or Munitions. Peaceable traffic of Civilian Population will not be restricted during daylight.

O.C. "D" Coy. is appointed picquetting Officer and will be required to find picquetts on Telegraphs and Telephone Offices, and Railway Stations under order of O.C. Advance Guard.

8. REPORTS. to head of Main Guard.

9. ADMINISTRATIVE ORDERS will be issued later.

10. THE BATTALION will be ready to move at 3 hours notice from receipt of this Order.
Packs will be concentrated at "C" Company Billet and placed in charge of the Quarter Guard, ready to load on lorries.

11. Acknowledge.

E. M. Hebbert.
Captain & Adjutant.
52nd. BATTALION DEVONSHIRE REGIMENT.

```
Copy No. 1 to    C.O.
  "   "  2  "    2nd. in Command.
  "   "  3  "    Adjutant.
  "   "  4  "    (A, B, C, & D) O's C. Coy.
  "   "  5  "    O.C., H.G.C.
  "   "  6  "    O.C., L.T.M.B.
  "   "  7  "    O.C., Cyclists Section.
  "   "  8  "    Battalion T.O.
  "   "  9  "    Quarter Master.
  "   " 10  "    War Diary.
  "   " 11  "    File.
  "   " 12 & 13  Spares.
```

Issued at _____2030_____ hours.

June 23/1919

52 Devon R

Army Form C. 2118.

WAR DIARY
or
INTELLIGENCE SUMMARY

(Erase heading not required.)

Instructions regarding War Diaries and Intelligence Summaries are contained in F. S. Regs., Part II. and the Staff Manual respectively. Title Pages will be prepared in manuscript.

Place	Date	Hour	Summary of Events and Information	Remarks and references to Appendices
BURSCHEID	1/7/19		Battalion moves back from SOLINGEN this morning and is now occupying its old stations in BURSCHEID and KUCKENBURG.	
"	4/7/19		To-day was observed as a Holiday in commemoration of the signing of Peace.	
DELLBRUCK.	5/7/19		Battalion moved to-day to DELLBRUCK for a ten day Musketry Course, and is encamped in Gravel Pits. Sheet 2 Germany 1/25000 Square Q 25.	
"	12/7/19		Battalion returned to BURSCHEID to-day, having completed an Annual Musketry Course, and held 1st, 2nd, and 3rd class Army Certificate examinations for the Battalion while at DELLBRUCK.	
B U R G	28/7/19.		Battalion moved to BURG for Perimeter duties in relief with the 1/5th. Battalion Devon Regt. Relief was completed by 14-00 hours and the dispositions of the Battalion are as follows:-

No. 1 Outpost Company RIGHT Sector. Capt. C.E. Cope, M.C. commanding "A" Coy. from Swimming Baths at WELLERSHAUSEN (inclusive) to ZURMUHLE (exclusive). Company Headquarters and 2 Platoons in support. Sheet 2 s S.W. 1/25000. Square 33.1.5. N.W. of WERMELSKIRCHEN.

CENTRE Sector.
No. 2 Outpost Company./Captain A.J. Castle M.M. commanding "B" Company, from ZURMUHLE inclusive to MILL POND, No. 9 Sentry Post 200 yards due E of KELLERSHAMMER Post inclusive. Coy. Headquarters SELLSCHEID (1 Platoon in support).

No. 3 Outpost Company. LEFT Sector, Captain A.F. Mills, M.C. commanding "C" Company (during absence of Capt. J.S. Hill, M.C. on leave) from No. 9 Sentry Post MILL POND (exclusive) to KAISER WILHELM Bridge half, (inclusive). (1 platoon in support). Coy. Headquarters WESTHAUSEN.

Battalion Headquarters and 1 Company in reserve, (Capt. L.B. Proctor, M.C. commanding "D" Coy.) at SCHLOSS; BURG. | |

[signature]
Lieut. Colonel
Bn. Devonshire Regt.

WAR DIARY
or
INTELLIGENCE SUMMARY

Army Form C. 2118.

(Erase heading not required.)

Instructions regarding War Diaries and Intelligence Summaries are contained in F. S. Regs., Part II. and the Staff Manual respectively. Title Pages will be prepared in manuscript.

Place	Date	Hour	Summary of Events and Information	Remarks and references to Appendices
URSCHEID	1/7/19		Battalion moves back from SOLINGEN this morning and is now occupying its old stations in BURSCHEID and KUCKENBURG.	
"	4/7/19		To-day was observed as a holiday in commemoration of the signing of Peace.	
ELLBRUCK.	5/7/19		Battalion moved to-day to DELLBRUCK for a ten day Musketry Course, and is encamped in Gravel Pits. Sheet 2 Germany 1/25000 Square Q.35.	
"	18/7/19		Battalion returned to BURSCHEID to-day, having completed an Annual Musketry Course, and held 1st, 2nd, and 3rd class Army Certificate examinations for the Battalion while at DELLBRUCK.	
U R G	28/7/19.		Battalion moved to BURG for perimeter duties in relief with the 1/5th. Battalion Devon Regt. Relief was completed by 14-00 hours and the dispositions of the Battalion are as follows:-	
			No. 1 Outpost Company RIGHT Sector. Capt. G.E. COPE, M.C. commanding "A" Coy. from Swimming Baths at MULLERSHAUSEN (inclusive) to ZURMUHLE (exclusive). Company Headquarters and 2 Platoons in support. Sheet 2 s. S.W. 1/25000. Square 55.1.5. N.W. of WERMELSKIRCHEN.	
			CENTRE Sector.	
			No. 2 Outpost Company. Captain A.J. Castle M.M. commanding "B" Company, from ZURMUHLE inclusive to MILL POND. No. 9 Sentry Post 200 yards due E of KELLERSHAMMER Post inclusive. Coy. Headquarters SELLSCHEID (1 Platoon in support).	
			No. 3 Outpost Company. LEFT Sector. Captain A.F. Mills, M.C. commanding "C" Company (during absence of Capt. J.S. Hill, M.O. on leave) from No. 9 Sentry Post MILL POND (exclusive) to KAISER WILHELM Bridge half (inclusive). Coy. Headquarters WESTHAUSEN, (1 platoon in support).	
			Battalion Headquarters and 1 Company in reserve, (Capt. L.B. Proctor, M.C. commanding "D" Coy.) at SCHLOSS BURG.	

Lieut. Colonel,
Bn. Devonshire Regt.

Army Form C. 2118.

WAR DIARY
or
INTELLIGENCE SUMMARY

(Erase heading not required.)

Instructions regarding War Diaries and Intelligence Summaries are contained in F. S. Regs., Part II. and the Staff Manual respectively. Title Pages will be prepared in manuscript.

Place	Date	Hour	Summary of Events and Information	Remarks and references to Appendices
BURSCHEID	1/7/19		Battalion moves back from SOLINGEN this morning and is now occupying its old stations in BURSCHEID and KUCKENBURG.	
"	4/7/19		To-day was observed as a Holiday in commemoration of the signing of Peace.	
DELLBRUCK.	5/7/19		Battalion moved to-day to DELLBRUCK for a ten day Musketry Course, and is encamped in Gravel Pits. Sheet 2 Germany 1/25000 Square Q.25.	
"	19/7/19		Battalion returned to BURSCHEID to-day, having completed an Annual Musketry Course, and held 1st, 2nd, and 3rd class Army Certificate examinations for the Battalion while at DELLBRUCK.	
B U R G	28/7/19.		Battalion moved to BURG for perimeter duties in relief with the 1/5th. Battalion Devon Regt. Relief was completed by 14-00 hours and the dispositions of the Battalion are as follows:-	
			No. 1 Outpost Company RIGHT Sector. Capt. C.E. Cope, M.C. commanding "A" Coy. from Swimming Baths at WETHLERSHAUSEN (inclusive) to ZURMUHLE (exclusive). Company Headquarters and 2 platoons in support. Sheet 2 s S.W. 1/25000. Square 53.1.5. N.W. of WERMELSKIRCHEN.	
			CENTRE sector.	
			No. 2 Outpost Company./Captain A.J. Castle M.M. commanding "B" Company, from ZURMUHLE inclusive to MILL POND, No. 9 Sentry Post 200 yards due E of KELLERSHAMMER Post inclusive. Coy. Headquarters SELLSCHEID (1 Platoon in support).	
			No. 3 Outpost Company. LEFT Sector, Captain A.F. Mills, M.C. commanding "C" Company (during absence of Capt. J.S. Hill, M.C. on leave) from No. 9 Sentry Post MILL POND (exclusive) to KAISER WILHELM Bridge half, (inclusive). Coy. Headquarters WESTHAUSEN, (1 platoon in support).	
			Battalion Headquarters and 1 Company in reserve, (Capt. L.B. Proctor, M.C. commanding "D" Coy.) at SCHLOSS, BURG.	

[signature]
Lieut. Colonel
Bn. Devonshire Regt.

Army Form C. 2118.

WAR DIARY
or
INTELLIGENCE SUMMARY.
(Erase heading not required.)

Instructions regarding War Diaries and Intelligence Summaries are contained in F. S. Regs., Part II. and the Staff Manual respectively. Title pages will be prepared in manuscript.

Place	Date	Hour	Summary of Events and Information	Remarks and references to Appendices
BURG	1/8/19	—	The Batt'n still held the Outpost Line as described in War Diary for July. Pay and Mess books scheme of accounting was commenced on 1st Aug. and RBs but withdrawn	

A.J.Shedden
Lieut. Colonel,
Comdg. 32nd Bn. Devonshire Regt.

Army Form C. 2118.

WAR DIARY
or
INTELLIGENCE SUMMARY.
(Erase heading not required.)

Instructions regarding War Diaries and Intelligence Summaries are contained in F. S. Regs., Part II. and the Staff Manual respectively. Title pages will be prepared in manuscript.

Place	Date	Hour	Summary of Events and Information	Remarks and references to Appendices
BURG	19.9		The Battn still holding Outpost Line.	
	22.9.9		One company withdrawn from perimeter and number of posts reduced to 8 and battalion front held by two companies instead of three.	
	27.9.9		Battalion relieved from Outpost line by 61st Br Devonshire Regt & proceeded to HILGEN with one company at TENTE.	

B. Schier, Lieut. Colonel
2nd Bn. Devonshire Regt.

52nd. BATTALION THE DEVONSHIRE REGIMENT.

MOVE TO HILGEN.

1. The 52nd. Battalion The Devonshire Regiment will be relieved on the Perimeter on the 27/9/19 by the 51st. Battalion The Devonshire Regiment, and on relief will occupy the billets vacated by the 51st Battalion The Devonshire Regiment.

   H.Q. & "C" Coy.   at   HILGEN.
   "A" Coy.   "   HILGEN.
   "B" Coy.   "   TENTE.
   "D" Coy.   "   NEUENHOUS.

   All correspondence, maps etc. relating to the defence and stores in charge on Perimeter will be handed over to incoming Unit and receipts obtained.

2. Breakfast will be as usual. Companies will arrange to have tea on arrival in new area, dinners will be at 17.00 hours.
   Companies will be ready for relief at 10.00 hours.

3. "A" & "C" Companies will move independently to new area on relief.
   H.Q. Band, "B" & "D" Companies and Transport will move off in relief in the order named with the head of the column at entrance to Hunger.
   Dress:- Full Marching Order.

4. All baggage and stores will be stacked ready for loading at 08.00 hours. Lorries on arrival with stores of the 51st Battalion The Devonshire Regiment will be reloaded and despatched with the least possible delay. O.C. Companies will detail one N.C.O. and three men, who are unable to march, to proceed with lorries and unload in Hilgen area. A guard will be provided from these men while lorries return for a second load.
   O.C. "C" Coy. will arrange to have all stores stacked in UNTER BURG under an armed guard on the 26th. Inst.

5. O.C. "D" Coy. will detail a party of one N.C.O. & 10 men to report to Transport Officer at 17.00 hours on 26th. inst.
   O.C. "B" Coy. will detail a loading party of 2 N.C.Os. & 20 men to report to Quartermaster at 08.00 hours 27th. inst.

6. All billets will be left clean and a certificate obtained from incoming Unit to this effect.

7. Relief to be completed by 10.00 hours. O.C. Companies will report relief complete to Battalion Headquarters.

                                    R. C. B L O O D W O R T H Lieutenant & Acting
                                                                        Adjutant
                                    52nd. Battalion The Devonshire Regiment.

Copy No. 1 to Commanding Officer.
  "   " 2   " Adjutant.
  "   " 3   " Quartermaster.
  "   " 4 to 8 O.C. "A" Coy.
  "   " 9 to 13 O.C. "B" Coy.
  "   " 14 to 18 O.C. "C" Coy.
  "   " 19 to 23 O.C. "D" Coy.
  "   "   24 to Transport Officer.
  "   "   25 " O.C. Civil Duties.
  "   "   26 " Education Officer.
  "   "   27 " Canteen.
  "   "   28 " Officers Mess.
  "   "   29 " Sergeants Mess.
  "   "   30 " Office File.
  "   "   31 " War Diary.
  "   "   32 " O.C. H.Q. Coy.
  "   "   33 " Medical Officer.
  "   "   34 " R.S.M.

Issued at 10-00 hours.   No:- 31.   War Diary

Army Form C. 2118.

WAR DIARY
or
INTELLIGENCE SUMMARY

(Erase heading not required.)

Instructions regarding War Diaries and Intelligence Summaries are contained in F. S. Regs., Part II. and the Staff Manual respectively. Title Pages will be prepared in manuscript.

Place	Date	Hour	Summary of Events and Information	Remarks and references to Appendices
HILGEN	21/10/1919		Two Companies took over BURG outpost line to-day. Headquarters Half Battalion established at SCHLOSS BURG under Major T.B. Jameson M.C.	
do	28/10/1919		Half Battalion on Burg outpost line relieved by 51st Battalion The Devonshire Regiment.	
BURSCHEID	31/10/1919		Battalion moved to BURSCHEID from HILGEN by road.	

BURSCHEID.
1/11/1919.

[signature]
Lieut-Colonel,
Commanding 52nd Bn The Devonshire Regiment.

52nd. BATTALION THE DEVONSHIRE REGIMENT.

BATTALION MOVE 31/10/19.

1. The 52nd. Battalion The Devonshire Regiment will move from Hilgen to Burscheid to morrow the 31/10/19.
   Billetts will be allotted on arrival by Billetting Officer 2/Lt., H.Horgan.

2. Breakfasts will be at 0700 hours. Dinners will be proved on arrival.

3. Battalion, less "C" and "A" Companies will parade outside Battalion Headquarters at 0950 hours, facing direction of Burscheid, in the following order. Headquarters, "B" "D". "A" Company will join rear of Column as the Battalion passes their Billetts. Band will parade with H.Q.Company.

   Dress:- Full Marching Order.

4. All Baggage and stores will be stacked ready for loading at 0800 hours outside Company Headquarters, Headquarter Company outside Battalion Orderly Room.
   Lorries are detailed as under:- (if available).
   FIRST TRIP.

   Two lorries to Quartermaster.
   One Lorry to Orderly Room and Canteen.
   One Lorry to "A" Company.

   SECOND TRIP.

   One Lorry to "B" Company.
   One Lorry to "D" Company.
   One Lorry to "A" Company.
   One lorry to Headquarters.

   THIRD TRIP.

   One Lorry to "D" Company.
   One Lorry to "B" Company.
   One lorry to Headquarters.
   One lorry to Quartermasters Stores.

5. O.C. "A" & "B" Companies will arrange to hand in any requisitioned stores (except expendable) not required on leaving Hilgen, to Sergt. Harvey at Quartermasters Stores, prior to moving off.
   O.C. "D" Company and Transport will hand in theirs to a billett to be arranged by "D" Company. O.C. "D" Company to detail an N.C.O. to take these stores in.
   List of stores so handed in to be prepared and forwarded together with location of billett stored in to Battalion Headquarters.

6. O.C. "A" Caompany will detail one N.C.O. and 10 men to report to R.Q.M.S. at 0800 hours. O.C. "B" Company will detail Sergt. Harvey to report to the Quartermaster to take over requision stores, and 6 men to report to Lieut Hayes at Cinema Hall at 0745 hours.

7. All Billetts will be left clean.

                                     W.CLARKE   Captain & Adjutant,
                           52nd. Bn. The Devonshire Regiment.

Issued At...1715...hours.
Copy No ..27.

Continued.

Copy No 1. To Commanding Officer.
" " 2. To Adjutant.
" " 3. To Quartermaster.
" " 4-8. O.C. "A" Company.
" " 9-13. O.C. "B" Company.
" " 14-18. O.C. "D" Company.
" " 19. O.C. "C" Company.
" " 20. To Billetting Officer.
" " 21. To Transport Officer.
" " 22. To Education Officer.
" " 23. To Canteen.
" " 24. To Officers Mess.
" " 25. To Sergts. Mess.
" " 26. To Office File.
" " 27. To War Diary.
" " 28. To O.C. Headquarter Company.
" " 29. To Medical Officer.
" " 30. To R.S.M.

ALARM ORDERS.

Copy No...11......

In the event of a rising or serious disturbance on part of the Civilian Population, the following action will be taken:-

1. (a) The Alarm will be sounded by the Battalion Headquarter Bugler on duty, and repeated by all Company Buglers who hear it.
   (b) A cyclist Orderly will be sent at once to each Company to carry the Alarm.
   (c) Troops will fall in on Company Alarm Posts.
       Dress, Fighting Order, Steel Helmets. Water bottles to be filled.

2. O.C. "C" Coy. will detail the following Guards:-

1 Platoon	HILGEN BRIDGE and WATER TOWER.
1 Platoon	HILGEN RAILWAY STATION. To furnish patrols 500x North and South of Station in addition to Guard.
1 Rifle Section	Battalion Quartermaster Stores.
1 Rifle Section	Civil Post Office.
1 Rifle Section	Civil Police Station.
1 Lewis Gun Section)	
1 Rifle Section)	Picquet at North end of HILGEN VILLAGE.
1 Lewis Gun Section	Picquet at South end of HILGEN VILLAGE.

   2 Rifle Sections under an Officer to patrol HILGEN VILLAGE, and enforce orders detailed under Para 4 "a" to "c".

3. Transport will concentrate in HILGEN near Battalion Headquarters, vehicles in Railway Station yard.

4. (a) All German Officials will be forced to remain at their posts and carry on with their duties under supervision.
   (b) All civilians will be confined to their houses, the Burgomaster issuing an order to that effect.
       Any civilians found in the streets without a pass signed by the O.C. Troops, will be arrested.
   (c) The movements of all trains and trams will be stopped.
   (d) Guards will be placed on all food and wine stores, and any persons attempting looting will be fired on.
       The Burgomaster will arrange for the proper distribution of food.

5. One Officer from each Company, accompanied by an Orderly, will report immediately to Battalion Headquarters.

6. All Headquarter Personnel not on duty will concentrate by Battalion Quarter Guard.

7. On hearing the "Alarm", action as detailed above will be taken.

[signature]

Lieut. Colonel,
Commanding 52nd. Battalion The Devonshire Regt.

Copy No. 1 to Commanding Officer.
"   " 2 " 2nd. I/Command.
"   " 3 " Adjutant.
"   " 4 " Quartermaster.
"   " 5 " "A" Coy.
"   " 6 " "B" "
"   " 7 " "C" "
"   " 8 " "D" "
"   " 9 " Transport Officer.
"   " 10 " O.C. "H.Q." Coy.
"   " 11 " War Diary.
"   " 12 " File.
"   " 13 " R.S.M.

52nd Battalion The Devonshire Regiment.
Movement Orders.

1. The Half Battalion, 52nd Battalion The Devonshire Regiment, will be relieved on the Perimeter on the 29/10/1919.

2. On relief billets will be occupied as under:-
"D" Company will take over the billets occupied by "B" Company in Hilgen before they proceeded to the perimeter.
"B" Company will take over "C" Company present billets.
"C" Company will take over billets vacated by "D" Company 51st Battalion The Devonshire Regiment at Burscheid.

All correspondence, maps etc relating to defence & stores on charge on Perimeter will be handed over to incoming unit & receipts obtained.

All requisitioned stores & all palliasses will be handed over to incoming unit & receipts obtained.

2. Breakfast for "B" & "D" Companies will be arranged by O.C. Half Battalion, & breakfast for "C" Company will be as usual. Companies will arrange for tea on arrival.

3. "B" & "D" Companies will move under orders of O.C.Detachment, Burg.

4. All baggage & stores will be stacked ready for loading under orders of O.C.Half Battalion. Lorries will report at 09.00 hours 29th inst.

5. Loading parties will be detailed by O.C.Half Battalion.

6. "C" Company will have baggage & stores stacked ready for loading at 09.00 hours. All palliasses will be taken over by incoming Company. A loading party of 1 N.C.O. & 5 men will be detailed by O.C. "C"Company, first unloaded from Outpost will pick up "C" Company's baggage & stores & convoy same to Burscheid.

7. O.C."C"Company will detail 1 Sergt, 1 Corpl & 6 men as a guard to relieve guard of 51st Battalion The Devonshire Regiment at Brigade Headquarters at Burscheid at 08.30 hours, & I N.C.O. & 3 men to relieve guard of 51st Battalion The Devonshire Regiment at R.E.Dump, Burscheid, at 08.30 hours. Bugler for Brigade Guard will be detailed from Battalion Headquarters to report to "C" Company.

8. All billets will be left clean & certificate obtained from incoming unit to this effect.

9. O.C.Companies will report relief complete to Battalion Headquarters.

W. C L A R K E. Captain & Adjutant.
52nd Battalion The Devonshire Regiment.

War Diary

52nd. Battalion The Devonshire Regiment.

MOVE.

Copy No. 16

B. and D. Coys. will proceed to Burg to-morrow to take over Perimeter from 51st. Battn. Devonshire Regiment. They will occupy RIGHT and LEFT SECTORS respectively of the BURG Outpost line.

One lorry will report to each of the two Company Headquarters concerned at 0800 hours to take up Company Stores, which should be ready for loading at that hour.

One N.C.O. and three men (unable to march) should accompany each of the lorries and unload on arrival.

Companies will ensure that the N.C.O. knows where the new Company Headquarters will be, so that he may guide the lorries.

Relief will be completed by 1500 hours. Companies will report relief to Major T.B.Jameson M.C. at Schloss Burg (Headquarters of Half Battalion) who will report to these Headquarters on completion.

All Billets will be examined and certified clean before marching out.

Lieut. R.C.Bloodworth will proceed with Major T.B.Jameson M.C. to Schloss Burg and will arrange to take over the necessary personnel for duty at Schloss, i.e, Signallers, Runners, Cook, Clerk & Batmen.

From & including Wednesday 22nd inst rations will be transported from Hilgen to Schloss Burg under arrangements made by the Quartermaster.

Outpost Companies will draw rations from Schloss on their Company Limbers as hitherto.

        E. N. H E B B E R T. Captain & Adjutant.
       52nd Battalion The Devonshire Regiment.
Issued at 11.00 Hours.
20/10/1919.

Copy No 1 to Commanding Officer.
 " " 2 " Major T.B.Jameson.M.C.
 " " 3 " Adjutant.
 " " 4 " Quartermaster.
 " " 5 " "A"Company.
 " "6-9 " "B" "
 " " 10 " "C" "
 " "11-14 "D" "
 " " 15 " File.
 " " 16 " War Diary.
 " " 17 " R.S.M.

ALARM ORDERS. (Amendment) Copy No. 11

1 (c) "A" Coy. will assemble in HILGEN STATION yard.

[signature] Capt. & Adjt.

Lieut.Colonel,
Commanding 52nd. Battalion The Devonshire Regiment.

```
Copy No.  1 to Commanding Officer.
  "    "  2  " 2nd. I/Command.
  "    "  3  " Adjutant.
  "    "  4  " Quartermaster.
  "    "  5  " "A" Company.
  "    "  6  " "B"    "
  "    "  7  " "C"    "
  "    "  8  " "D"    "
  "    "  9  " Transport Officer.
  "    " 10  " O.C."H.Q." Coy.
  "    " 11  " War Diary.
  "    " 12  " File.
  "    " 13  " R.S.M.
```

www.ingramcontent.com/pod-product-compliance
Lightning Source LLC
Chambersburg PA
CBHW081500160426
43193CB00013B/2544